PIANO · VOCAL · GUITAR

EMELI SANDÉ LONG LIVE THE ANGELS

ISBN 978-1-4950-8266-5

7777 W. BLUEMOUND RD. P.O. BOX 13819 MILWAUKEE, WI 53213

In Australia Contact:
Hal Leonard Australia Pty. Ltd.
4 Lentara Court
Cheltenham, Victoria, 3192 Australia
Email: ausadmin@halleonard.com.au

Visit Hal Leonard Online at
www.halleonard.com

BABE

Words by EMELI SANDÉ
Music by EMELI SANDÉ,
MATTHEW HOLMES and PHILIP LEIGH

BREATHING UNDERWATER

Words by EMELI SANDÉ
Music by EMELI SANDÉ
and CHRIS CROWHURST

GARDEN

Words by EMELI SANDÉ
Music by EMELI SANDÉ, CHRIS CROWHURST,
TIMOTHY THEDFORD and AINE ZION

Spoken 1 (See Additional Lyrics)

Let me love,   let me touch, let me love, ba - by, give it up;   let me
in the club;   how you dance, how you touch, how you of - fer up   all your
make it real,   make me feel, make me feel I'm as strong as steel   and as

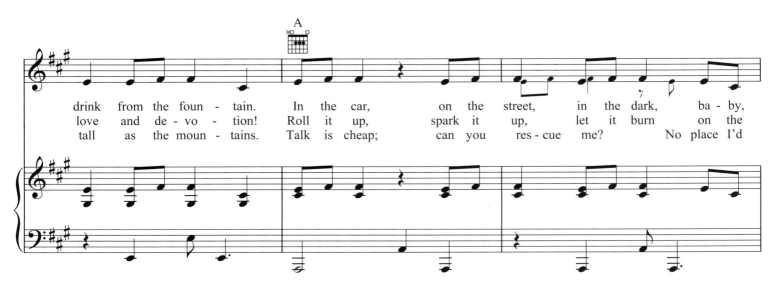

drink from the foun - tain. In the car,   on the street, in the dark, ba - by,
love and de - vo - tion! Roll it up, spark it up, let it burn on the
tall as the moun - tains. Talk is cheap; can you res - cue me? No place I'd

Rap (See Additional Lyrics)

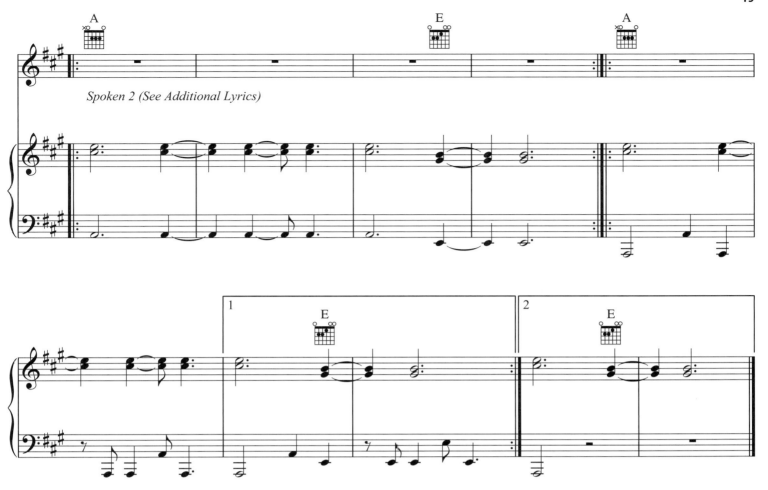

Spoken 2 (See Additional Lyrics)

Additional Lyrics

Spoken 1:   I'm not telling you to love what I love; I'm asking you to take time to know
what it is that you love and are in love with. And do what you can not to offend this sensitive soul. You have seen things
no lips can confess, no pain can bear witness to, no mind can justify, no memory can wipe.

Rap: Once upon a time ago, I threw my cautions to the wind, my friend,
And yelled, "Geronimo!" and rode the wings of love to outer space.
But then I fell a thousand miles to Guantanamo.
Euphoria to torture. I left a note that had a rhyme, it go:

Love is like the Ferris wheel; love is like a roller coaster;
Love is at a standstill. Body after body after body,
It's a landfill. And I just caught a body in the lobby
And got my hands filled. I'm a serial lover.

I set up all the dates that rang up fate and got my friends killed.
I barely knew my dad; sometimes I feel like my mother
I love that Purple Rain love... That have a fight, that scratch my face,
That fuck outside and ride my motorcycle in the rain love.

Love is like a garden; love is like a death sentence.
Love is like a pardon; I'm free again and ready.
Once outside these prison walls, to believe again is scary.
Your garden is my sanctuary. (Back of the garden.)

Spoken 2:   Be my confidant, my shoulder, my diary, my best friend, my mentor, my lover, my teacher,
my preacher, my one and only, my everything. From the beam of the sun to the dim of the moon,
from before until always, I'm yours. So keep me safe within yourself. Bow to my throne,
no matter what, and I will stand tall.

EVERY SINGLE LITTLE PIECE

Words by EMELI SANDÉ
Music by EMELI SANDÉ, PHILIP LEIGH
and MATTHEW HOLMES

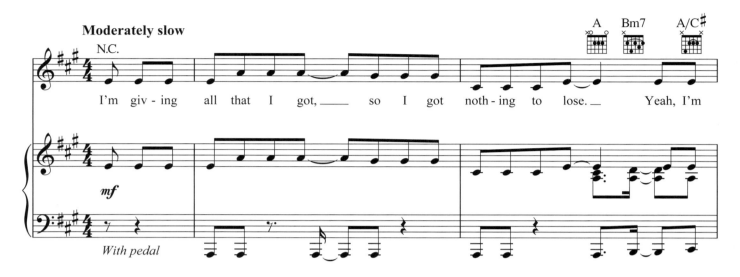

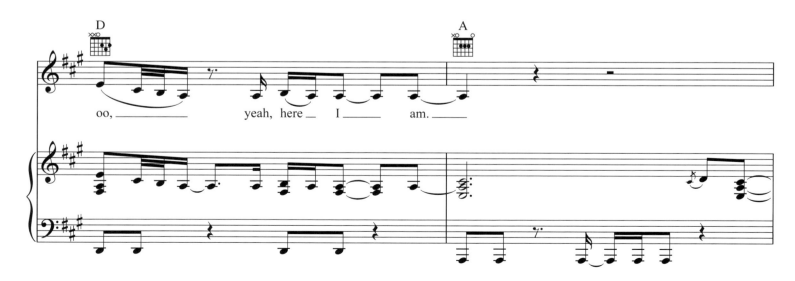

GIVE ME SOMETHING

Words by EMELI SANDÉ
Music by EMELI SANDÉ, PHILIP LEIGH,
MATTHEW HOLMES and CHRIS CROWHURST

Slow half-time shuffle

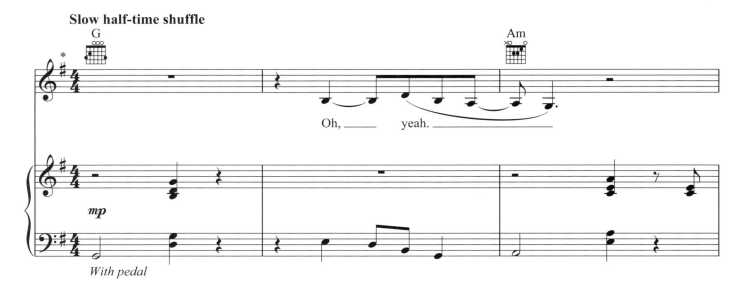

With pedal

Oh, ___ yeah. ___

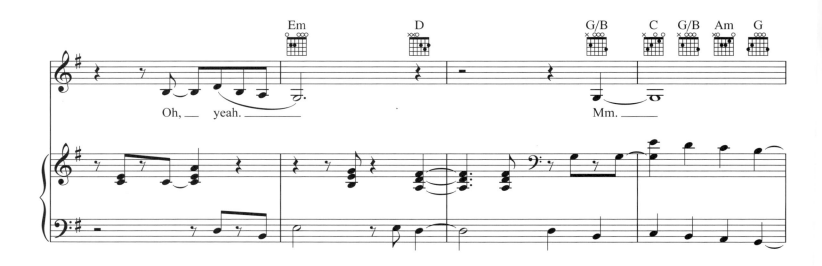

Oh, ___ yeah. ___ Mm. ___

I guess I got caught up   in the rough ___ and tum-

* *Recorded a half step lower.*

HAPPEN

Words by EMELI SANDÉ
Music by EMELI SANDÉ, MATTHEW HOLMES,
PHILIP LEIGH, SHAHID KHAN
and JONATHAN COFFER

Recorded a half step higher.

HIGHS & LOWS

Words by EMELI SANDÉ
Music by EMELI SANDÉ, BENJAMIN KOHN,
PETER KELLEHER, THOMAS BARNES
and WAYNE HECTOR

HURTS

Words by EMELI SANDÉ
Music by EMELI SANDÉ, PHILIP LEIGH,
MATTHEW HOLMES, JAMES MURRAY
and MUSTAFA OMER

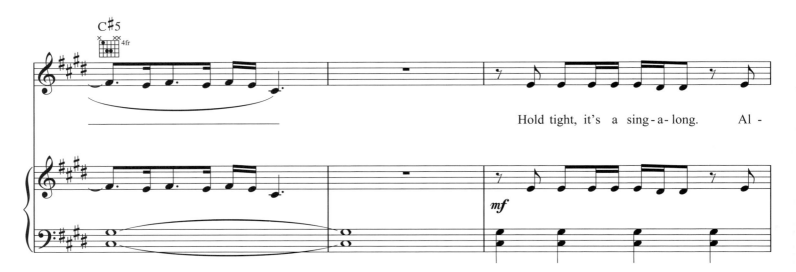

I'D RATHER NOT

Words by EMELI SANDÉ
Music by EMELI SANDÉ, SHAHID KHAN,
SHAKIL ASHRAF and JONATHAN COFFER

Moderate groove

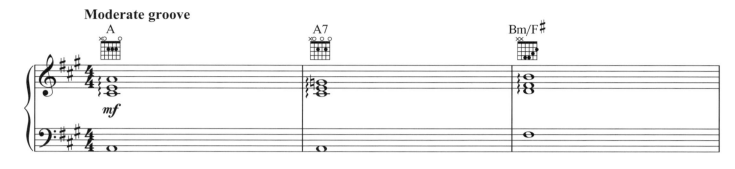

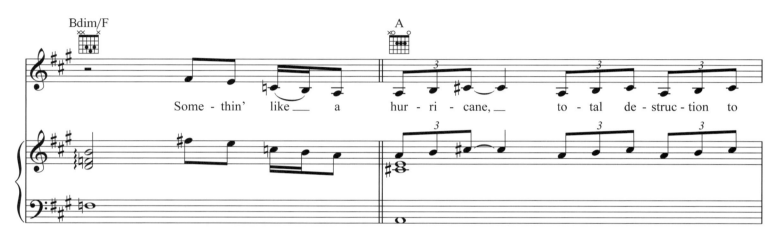

Some - thin' like ___ a hur - ri - cane, ___ to - tal de - struc - tion to

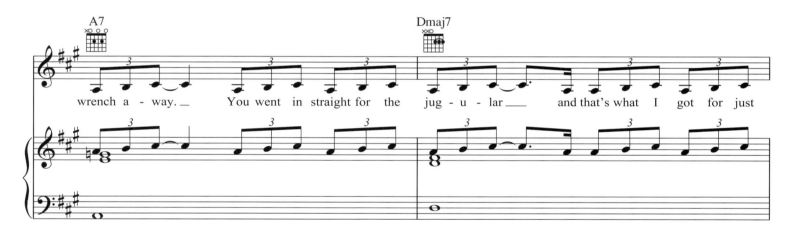

wrench a - way. ___ You went in straight for the jug - u - lar ___ and that's what I got for just

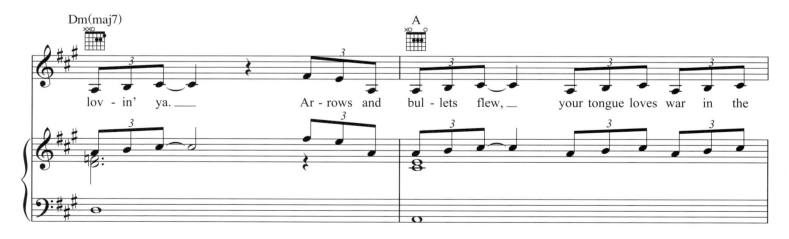

lov - in' ya. ___ Ar - rows and bul - lets flew, ___ your tongue loves war in the

No, I can't make it stop ___ but I'd rath-er not, I'd rath-er not. ___

(Lead vocal ad lib.)

LONELY

Words by EMELI SANDÉ
Music by EMELI SANDÉ, PHILIP LEIGH,
MATTHEW HOLMES, JAMES MURRAY
and MUSTAFA OMER

RIGHT NOW

Words by EMELI SANDÉ
Music by EMELI SANDÉ, MATTHEW HOLMES,
PHILIP LEIGH and SHAHID KHAN

Gently, poco rubato

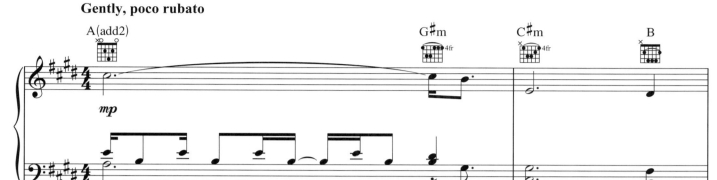

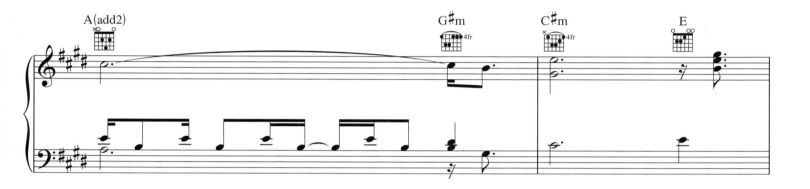

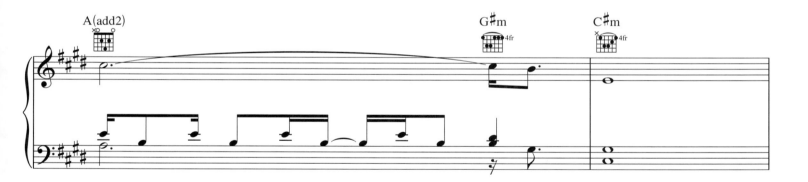

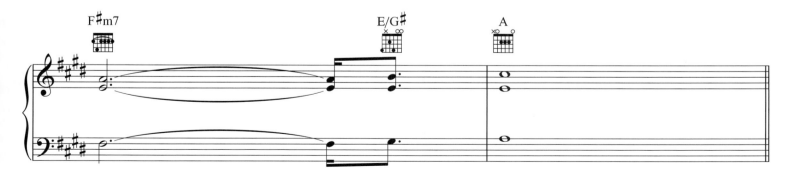

64

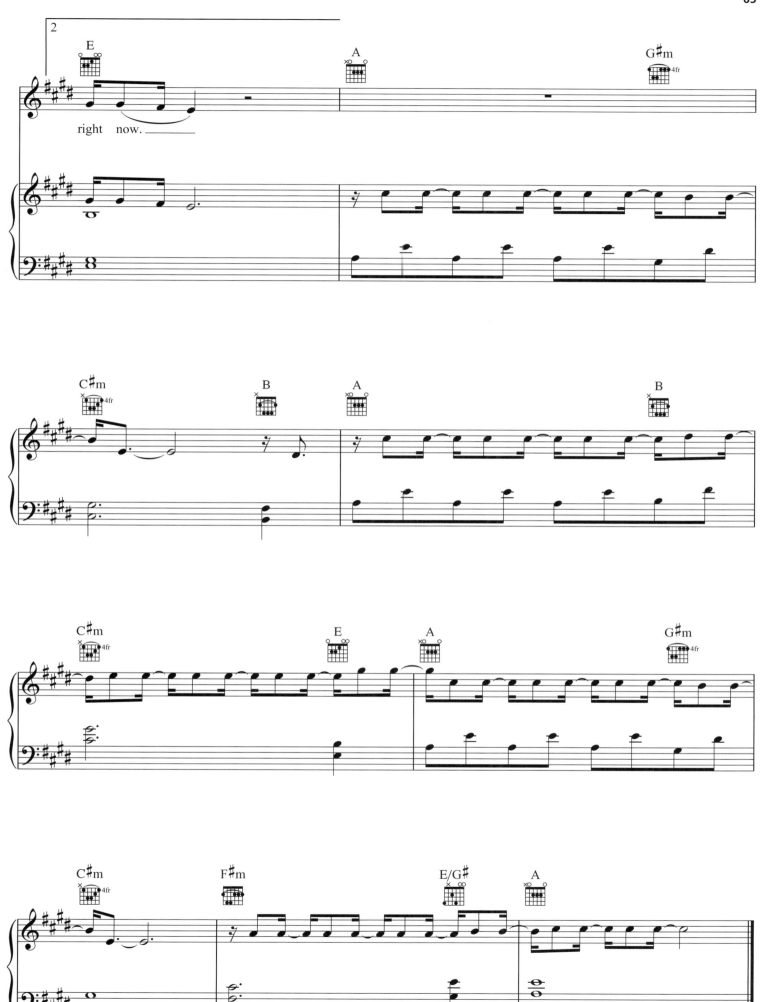

right now.

SELAH

Words and Music by
EMELI SANDÉ

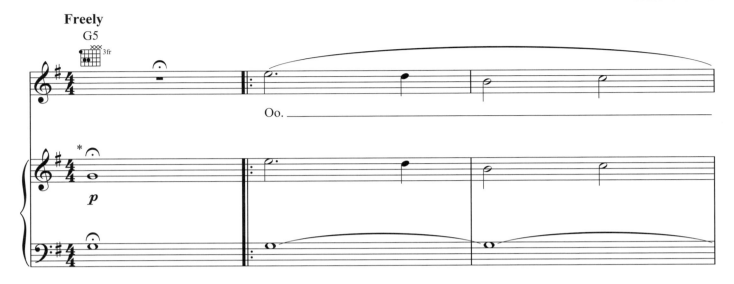

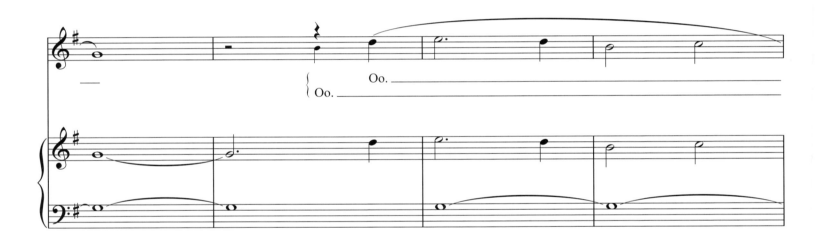

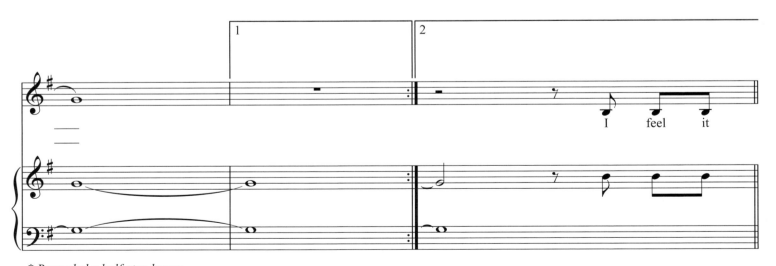

* *Recorded a half-step lower*

SHAKES

Words by EMELI SANDÉ
Music by EMELI SANDÉ and SHAHID KHAN

Slow Ballad

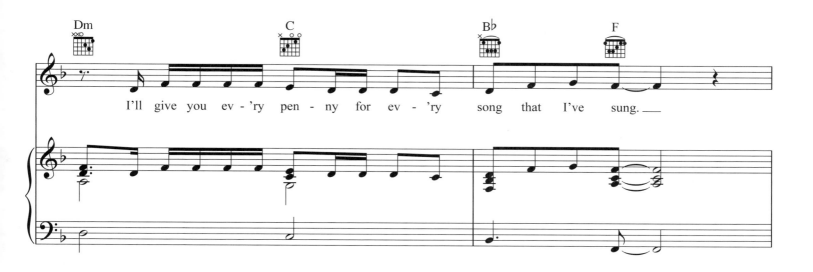

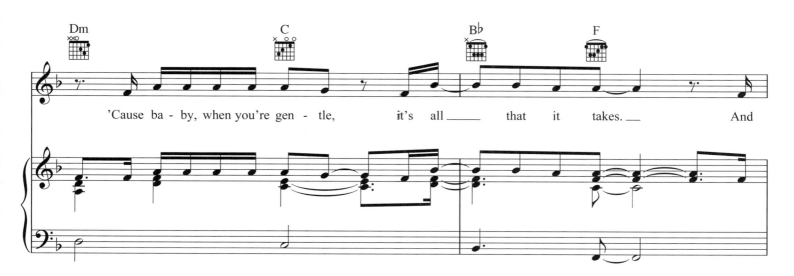

SWEET ARCHITECT

Words by EMELI SANDÉ
Music by EMELI SANDÉ, JAMES MURRAY,
MUSTAFA OMER and JONATHAN COFFER

Piano Ballad

Oh, sweet ar - chi - tect, __ my bones are heav-y and my soul's a mess. __ Can't find

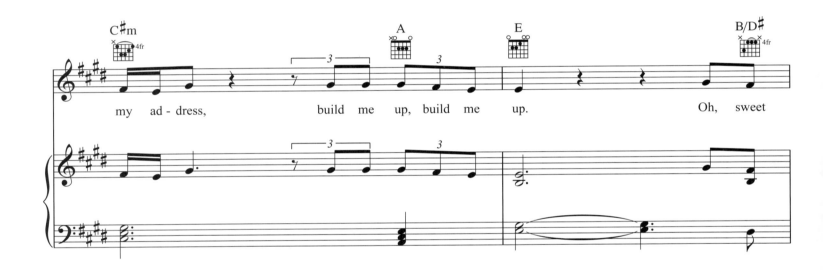

my ad - dress, build me up, build me up. Oh, sweet

ar - chi - tect, __ I've been lone - ly since the day you left. __ So, come find

TENDERLY

Words by EMELI SANDÉ
Music by EMELI SANDÉ, MATTHEW HOLMES,
PHILIP LEIGH and JOEL SANDÉ

tough e - nough.
like to play rough.

So ba - by, love me ten - der - ly.

1, 2, 3

4

Oh, why don't you ___ just
(Sing 1st time only)

Vocal ad lib.

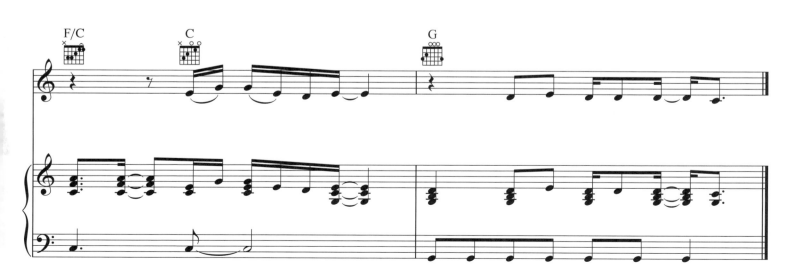